W9-ASZ-969

AUTHORS TEENS LOVE

Gary Paulsen

Voice of Adventure and Survival

JoAnn Early Macken

Enslow Publishers, Inc.
40 Industrial Road
Box 398
Berkeley Heights, NJ 07922
USA
http://www.enslow.com

Copyright © 2008 by JoAnn Early Macken

All rights reserved.

No part of this book may be reproduced by any means without the written permission of the publisher.

Library of Congress Cataloging-in-Publication Data

Macken, JoAnn Early, 1953–
    Gary Paulsen : voice of adventure and survival / JoAnn Early Macken.
        p. cm. — (Authors teens love series)
    Includes bibliographical references and index.
    ISBN-13: 978-0-7660-2721-3
    ISBN-10: 0-7660-2721-X
    1. Paulsen, Gary. 2. Authors, American—20th century—Biography—
Juvenile literature. 3. Adventure and adventurers—United
States—Biography—Juvenile literature. 4. Young adult fiction—
Authorship—Juvenile literature. I. Title.
    PS3566.A834Z77 2006
    813'.54—dc22
    [B]
                                            2006022849

Printed in the United States of America

10 9 8 7 6 5 4 3 2 1

To Our Readers: We have done our best to make sure all Internet addresses in this book were active and appropriate when we went to press. However, the author and publisher have no control over and assume no liability for the material available on those Internet sites or on other Web sites they may link to. Any comments or suggestions can be sent by e-mail to comments@enslow.com or to the address on the back cover.

Illustration Credits: AP/Wide World Photos, pp. 41, 48, 52, 80; Courtesy of JoAnn Early Macken, pp. 4, 59, 68, 76; Shutterstock Inc., pp. 29, 33.

Cover Illustration: Courtesy of JoAnn Early Macken (photo), and Michael Findlay (background art).

CONTENTS

CHAPTER 1

"You Use What You Are"

Plenty of daring people had plunged over Niagara Falls in barrels. Twelve-year-old Gary Paulsen had read about them in a magazine. Most of them had died trying, but that fact was far from his young mind. He was thinking of fame and glory.

He found an old pickle barrel and taped the sides together. He bound the barrel with rope and stuffed a quilt inside to cushion his fall. When he climbed in and lowered the lid, it sealed tightly. Then he wiggled his way into the river. He thought the current would carry him over the dam and the twelve-foot waterfall.

The barrel sank like a cannonball, straight to the bottom—with Gary inside.

To his horror, he found the lid stuck tight. The sides were reinforced—he had made sure of that. As he kicked and fought, water poured in through the cracks. Luckily for him, the current picked up the barrel at last. As the barrel tumbled over the dam, Gary rattled around inside. The barrel plunged over the falls and shattered on a sharp rock. His nose was bleeding, but he was alive.

Paulsen describes the stunt, his introduction to boating, along with other escapades from his childhood, in *How Angel Peterson Got His Name: And Other Outrageous Tales About Extreme Sports*.

When he was older, Paulsen spent almost a week on the coast of California after he left the army. "I sat down," he said, "and let the sea heal me." After that peaceful time, he thought of himself as a new person. "I also began to understand things about myself, that I must see and know the oceans. I must go to the sea." Like Herman Melville and other writers, he said, "I must seek myself there."[1]

Later, when Paulsen finally learned how to sail, he learned the hard way. Soon after he bought a small sailboat, he decided to try it out. He went for a sail alone on the Pacific Ocean. When he left the harbor, he had no idea how much adventure lay ahead.

Twelve miles from shore, huge waves rose up, and the boat began to rock. Then a strong wind blew the boat sideways. Scared and alone, with water pouring over him, Paulsen hung on. The boat was out of control, and he did not know what to do. He just knew he had to save the boat to survive.

Paulsen decided his only option—impossible as

it seemed—was to lower the sails. He found a loose rope, looped it under his arms, and tied himself to the boat. He thought he could pull himself up if he fell overboard. Each time the mainsail bounced up out of the water, he crept forward. As the boat pitched and rolled, he loosened the mainsail and pulled it down. The boat rolled upward with the sail still dragging, and water poured in.

The pressure let up when the mainsail came down, but the wind still pulled the boat along. The forward sail had to come down, too. In the wind, the boom, the pole that held the bottom of the mainsail, swung back and forth wildly. It smacked into Paulsen and dragged him out over the water. He hung there until he was swept back over the boat and could put his feet down. At last, he fastened the mainsail and tied another rope from his waist to the mast. He crawled out to take down the forward sail. As night fell, the wind and waves grew more intense. Exhausted, he almost gave up hope.

The next morning, Paulsen realized he was lost. He had a compass, and he knew he had to sail east to reach land. He did not know that the wind and current had carried him two hundred fifty miles. Then the wind quit, and all he could do was wait. When the wind appeared again on the fifth day, he sailed as long as he could keep his eyes open. He woke to find himself far off course. By trial and error, he figured out how to adjust the sails to keep heading in the right direction.

From sailing to dogsled racing to motorcycle

riding, Gary Paulsen is still the kind of person who plunges into adventures before asking questions. That trait makes his writing authentic and earns him fans of all ages. Paulsen does not just venture out into the world. He uses his experiences to fuel his work. In order to make his writing come alive, he always tries to experience what his characters do. "You use what you are," he once said.[2]

Sailing is not only an adventure for Paulsen, but also a subject he has tackled in several books. In *The Voyage of the Frog*, fourteen-year-old David Alspeth inherits a sailboat from his uncle. While sailing alone, David notices a change in the waves. He realizes the wind has picked up. Just in time, he takes down the sails and stuffs them into the cabin. As the *Frog* tilts sideways, the boom swings across the boat and slams into David's head. Water pours into the cabin until he forces himself to get up and close the hatch. He has to pump out the water, straighten the sails, and hoist them back up. He leaves the wet cushions and gear in the sun to dry. While he waits for the wind to pick up, he washes himself off, takes stock of his food and water, and cleans out the cabin.

> **In order to make his writing come alive, he always tries to experience what his characters do.**

Just as Paulsen did, David tries fishing but has

no luck. Like Paulsen, he finds himself two hundred fifty miles from home. He also faces some of the same dangers Paulsen faced, including a shark attack and a shortage of food. In addition, the enormous wake of a passing oil tanker nearly sinks the *Frog*. Finally, after several days, the wind picks up, and he sails toward home. A review in *School Library Journal* said of *The Voyage of the Frog*, "Paulsen's spare prose offers an affecting blend of the boy's inner thoughts and keen observations of the power of nature to destroy and to heal."[3]

Paulsen now knows more about boats than just how to sail them. He also maintains his own boat. "There is in some strange way an almost sacred satisfaction in working on boats," he said.[4] He has used his sailing experience to write nonfiction as well. In *Sailing, from Jibs to Jibing*, he provides sailing instructions and information about equipment. He explains what to do in an emergency and how to care for and repair a sailboat.

Working on boats has brought him a great deal of satisfaction. "Each thing I did with complete attention as you must with a boat, forgetting career, family, everything; days on days working on the boat as if I were fixing my body, which in a measure I suppose I was, boats being such a complete extension of the sailor," Paulsen said.[5] He would rather be with dogs or on his sailboat than any other place on earth.

As he wrote in *My Life in Dog Years*, "I am—I say this with some pride and not a little wonder—a 'dog person.'"

Where Gary Paulsen's Ideas Come From

Paulsen's book *Hatchet* is a thrilling story about a thirteen-year-old boy who is stranded in the Canadian wilderness after a plane crash. Brian Robeson has to figure out how to find food, make a shelter, and build a fire alone. Brian's story continues in *The River, Brian's Winter, Brian's Return,* and *Brian's Hunt.* About *Hatchet,* Paulsen said, "I have been in forced landings in light planes and had to survive in the woods with little or nothing; virtually everything that happens to Brian in the book has happened in one form or another to me, just in the process of living." [6]

Paulsen kept getting letters from readers asking where he got his ideas for *Hatchet* and the other stories about Brian Robeson. To answer them, he wrote *Father Water, Mother Woods: Essays on Fishing and Hunting in the North Woods.* In this book, he describes what he learned from the time he spent in the woods growing up. Paulsen explains that the experiences of his own life informed his writing. In the Minnesota woods, he escaped from an abusive family life. "I would go to the woods," he said, "and I would hide. And I would trap or fish. Or I would go to uncles' farms. All over northern Minnesota were people I was related to, and they were glad to have me. It was free labor, and I would live on their farms. And a lot of that I write about now, too, of course, involves working on a farm as a teen. But I am lucky I survived." [7]

Even after the book of essays was published, Paulsen's readers were not satisfied. They wanted more details. Had Paulsen lived through a plane crash himself? How did he know so much about survival in the wilderness? To answer those questions, Paulsen wrote *Guts: The True Stories Behind Hatchet and the Brian Books*. He describes two near plane crashes in Alaska and how he recalled the sensations he felt during those incidents to write *Hatchet*. Brian's moose attack is based on Paulsen's own encounters with moose. Paulsen also explains how he made his own bows and arrows and used them for hunting.

To make sure the books were authentic, Paulsen tried everything Brian did. "When I set out to write the Brian books I was concerned that everything that happened to Brian should be based on reality, or as near reality as fiction could be. I did not want him to do things that wouldn't or couldn't really happen in his situation," he explained. "Consequently I decided to write only of things that had happened to me or things I purposely did to make certain they would work for Brian."[8] For the sake of research, Paulsen tasted grubs, fish eyes, snakes, and seal blood. He ate brains from a variety of wild creatures. His books are based on solid personal experience.

As James A. Schmitz wrote in an article in *The ALAN Review*, "Gary Paulsen writes award-winning survival stories and does it as good as anyone in the business. But the best of his survival tales is his own, the one you find spread through his books."[9]

"I make no excuses for unabashedly loving [dogs]—all of them, even some that have bitten me. I have always had dogs and will have dogs until I die. I have rescued dozens of dogs from pounds, always have five or six of them around me, and cannot imagine living without dogs."[10]

Writers are often told to write about what they know. The success of Paulsen's work shows the wisdom of this advice. Besides dogs and sailing, other aspects of Paulsen's life are reflected in his books. Many of his books have common characteristics: rural settings; memories from the narrator's youth; relationships with sympathetic adults, some of whom are relatives; alcoholic parents; adults who suffer from the effects of war; and boys who learn about life and death through struggles with animals or nature.

All these characteristics in his books spring from Paulsen's own life. At one time, he says, he believed in "the concept that personal inspection at ground zero is the only way to learn something. And I lived that way, and it's been very hard—I mean I've broken my bones—and I've been in trouble physically and mentally and all those things doing it. But I would not recommend it. . . . It's not necessarily a good way to learn to be a writer at all. It's just my way."[11]

Paulsen does not venture out just to find material; he does what he wants to do. "I have lived and trapped in the bush and have twice run the Iditarod dogsled race—indeed I have over twenty thousand miles on sleds—and have hunted when I wanted and fished when I wanted and played poker when I wanted and taken horses on long pack trips when I wanted. . . . I have had a life of such good fortune and seeming looseness that many who knew me or of me envy what they term my 'freedom,'" he said. And yet, "I was never really loose. I lunged on the chain and stretched it, slammed against the pull of it but could never break it. Always it jerked me back until I would pace and walk the end like a cat in a cage—my own chain, my own cage—until I had rested enough or gathered enough strength or courage or desperation, whatever it was I needed and then out again."[12] He is as driven to test himself and his boundaries as he is committed to writing about his experiences.

Paulsen hopes one day to sail alone around Cape Horn, the southernmost tip of South America.

Paulsen continues his adventures by dogsled and motorcycle as well as on sailboats. His current boat is equipped with solar panels that charge golf cart batteries. That system runs his laptop computer so he can write while he sails. During one long trip, he wrote four books!

Paulsen hopes one day to sail alone around Cape Horn, the southernmost tip of South America. To prepare for the long and dangerous journey, he has sailed to Hawaii, Samoa, Tonga, and Fiji. Another trip took him to Mexico and the Sea of Cortez. "I know that my life on boats has been about this: not the sailing or the sea so much as learning about self," he said. "And almost every boat I have had has taught me something." He planned his voyages "to show me the sea. To show me myself. And never, ever to look back."[13]

CHAPTER 2

Wartime and a Military Family

In 1939, the year Gary Paulsen was born, World War II began. The war shaped the lives of many people, including those of the Paulsen family.

Gary's father's family had come to the United States from Denmark. His mother's family came from Norway and Sweden. Gary's parents met in Minnesota. His father, Oscar, who was an army officer, had come from Kansas to Fort Snelling, near Minneapolis. Gary was born on May 17, 1939. Shortly after Gary was born, his father left for more training with the army. The United States entered the war in 1941. Oscar Paulsen traveled to Africa and Europe as an officer on the staff of General George Patton.

Gary and his mother, Eunice, lived in an apartment in Minneapolis for several years. Although he wrote letters from time to time, Gary's father never managed to spend enough time at home to get to know his son.

As a child, Gary was often sick. At that time, illnesses that are now considered minor often killed people. Antibiotics were not available, so many people died from infections. Gary once had appendicitis on a train trip from Chicago to Minneapolis. Several times, he suffered from colds that turned into pneumonia. Many years later, he remembered his mother holding his hand while he was in an oxygen tent in a hospital. Doctors thought he would die.

When Gary was four years old, his mother took him by train to northern Minnesota. His cousin was sick, and the two families spent Christmas together. The book *A Christmas Sonata* is based on that trip. It tells the story of two cousins, one visiting the other who is dying. The boys wonder about Santa Claus and his reindeer, waiting to see whether they will appear on Christmas Eve.

Soon after that trip, Gary's mother found a job in Chicago, Illinois. She worked in a factory making ammunition for the war. Because she worked at night, she hired a woman to watch Gary. As he wrote later, "she did not read to me or cook for me or hold me or cuddle me. She sat."[1] They spent much of their time listening to radio programs while the woman drank glass after glass of red wine.

Late at night, his mother came home, often with a treat for Gary. At first, she would talk to him when she got home, telling him about her job and the people she worked with. Then she began coming home later and later. Gary was often asleep by the time she got to the apartment. Sometimes he thought she smelled like beer, and he did not like the smell.

On weekends when his mother did not work, she took Gary to a nearby tavern for dinner. Gary wore a little army uniform, and people paid him to sing. His mother danced with men at the tavern. Gary was afraid of these men and hated spending so much time at the tavern. One day, his mother told Gary that one of the men would be moving into their apartment with them. She told Gary to call him "Uncle Casey."

Soon after the man moved in, Gary was sent to live with his grandmother. His book *The Cookcamp* is based on that summer. He has said that the story is virtually nonfiction.

In *The Cookcamp*, a boy travels alone on a train from Chicago to northern Minnesota. His grandmother works there as a cook for a group of nine huge men who are building a road to Canada. The boy spends the summer with his grandmother, helping her cook on a woodburning stove. In the cook trailer, the boy sets the tables and serves food to the men. He takes their empty plates away and helps wash the dishes. He wipes down the tables and sweeps the floor. Outside, he watches chipmunks and builds a tiny town out of dirt and sticks.

Slowly, he makes friends with the men who "made him think of big, polite bears."[2] They ruffle his hair and take him along to ride on tractors, bulldozers, and dump trucks as they build the road. As the road is built, they have to keep moving the trailers where they eat and sleep so they can stay close to their work.

Although the boy finally feels at home in the cook camp, he misses his mother. His grandmother writes to her and arranges for him to return home. Like the boy in the book, Gary Paulsen rode the train back to Chicago at the end of the summer. The man he called "Uncle Casey" lived with him and his mother until the end of the war.

When World War II ended, people celebrated by dancing in the streets. Gary's father wrote to his mother about his work with General Patton and the places he had seen. In a letter, he broke the news that he would not be coming home. Instead, he would be working in the Philippine Islands. He had made arrangements for Gary and his mother to take a ship from San Francisco and join him there.

Getting to San Francisco was a problem because so many people were traveling at the same time. Some were coming home from the war. Others were going to meet people coming home. All the trains were full. People waited in train stations for days to buy tickets.

If Gary and his mother had to wait for a train, they would miss their ship. They found a ride with two soldiers and drove across the country in a 1940 Ford sedan.

After several days in the car, Gary was sick— hot, weak, and throwing up. His mother found spots all over his body. Before they reached San Francisco, he had chicken pox.

People who travel to other countries often need shots so they do not catch diseases. Before he could leave for the Philippines, Gary saw a doctor. The doctor said Gary was not supposed to leave

> **A plane was about to crash into the ocean near the ship. . . . As it hit the water, the plane broke apart, and people in life vests crawled out onto the wing.**

the country until the chicken pox spots cleared up. But he did not tell anyone Gary was sick. Gary's mother met with the captain of the ship, and they carried him onboard at night, wrapped in a blanket, so no one would see him.

After nine days on the ship, Gary was allowed to leave his cabin. As he found his way up to the deck, he saw men lowering a rescue boat into the water. A plane was about to crash into the ocean near the ship.

The ship's engines stopped. Crowds of people filled the deck to watch. As it hit the water, the plane broke apart, and people in life vests crawled out onto the wing.

As the observers on the ship watched in horror, a school of sharks attacked the plane crash survivors. Many of them disappeared. The rescue boats returned with injured survivors, and Gary's mother helped care for them. Gary found a boy who had lost his mother in the attack and brought him along as he explored the ship.

The plane had departed from Hawaii, so the ship stopped there to drop off the injured passengers. It made another stop in Japan to drop off many of the sailors onboard. Finally, they arrived in the Philippines.

In Manila, a sergeant picked them up in a jeep and drove them past buildings that had been destroyed in the war. They drove on a road full of craters made by bombs and mines. They drove past shacks made of cardboard, wooden crates, and pieces of metal.

They drove through the gate in a high fence topped with barbed wire. Guards holding machine guns watched from tall towers. Their new home, inside the fence, stood three feet off the ground on stilts. The walls were woven bamboo on the bottom and screens on top. Gary found a world different from anything he had known. Lizards crawled through the house. Banana trees grew in the yard. A mean pet monkey lived next door.

His new life was different too. At last, Gary met his father, a tall, serious man he recognized from pictures. Gary was seven years old.

Slowly, the family settled into a new way of life. Gary started school, but he never spent much time in classes. He met with a tutor four times a week. Gary's mother made friends with the wives of other army officers. They played cards or held parties at the officers' club. As Gary's mother got to know the other women better, she was gone more often. She also drank more and more.

Gary saw his father for only a short time each evening. Even at seven years old, Gary sensed that he and his father would never be close.

His mother began meeting his father after

Leaving the fenced military area was strictly forbidden, but his parents never found out about these adventures.

work, and then they both came home after Gary was in bed. The family had two servants in Manila, a young man named Rom and a young woman named Maria. When his parents were gone, Gary was left in the servants' care.

Besides the rows of houses, the fenced-in area included a water tower, an airstrip, open fields, several larger buildings, and areas full of wrecked military equipment. Gary spent much of his time with Rom, exploring the area inside the fence. Rom built a seat for Gary to sit on his bicycle, and they rode around together. They watched soldiers marching. They played in ruined tanks and planes.

The jungle outside grew almost to the fence. One day, Gary watched a water buffalo working in the rice paddies. He talked Rom into taking him outside the fence to ride on it. Leaving the fenced military area was strictly forbidden, but his parents never found out about these adventures.

On a vacation in the mountains, the family

found a dog that was about to be killed and eaten. Gary talked his mother into buying it. He named the dog "Snowball" because of a round white spot on her side. For a time, Snowball became his best friend. She slept inside the mosquito netting on Gary's bed. She followed Gary as he explored the city and countryside. She even saved his life once by killing a poisonous snake. The story is included in *My Life in Dog Years*. One day as Gary walked with Snowball, a truck full of Filipino soldiers drove by and ran over the dog. It seemed to Gary that they did it on purpose. Once again, he was alone.

After two years in the Philippines, Gary could speak some of the Filipino language. He spent his days with Rom, riding around on the bicycle and exploring the neighborhoods outside the fence. His parents drank every night, and the more they drank, the more they fought.

His mother could not stand her life in the Philippines. Finally, in early 1949, she and Gary flew back to the United States. Gary's father followed them. He worked at the Pentagon for about nine months, and the family lived in Washington, D.C., until he retired from the army.

CHAPTER 3

Escaping From Troubles

After his father's military service was over, Gary's family moved again. They returned to Minnesota to raise chickens on a small farm. Gary's parents still drank heavily and fought often.

From time to time, Gary stayed with relatives. As he put it, "I was reared by my grandmother and several aunts." He has called them his "safety nets."

"There were also my uncles and aunts, who were all Scandinavian," he said. "Although they didn't think of themselves as storytellers, they would sit and talk, and tell about their youth and about things they had seen. I loved listening to them, and what they told *were* stories, beautiful stories."[1]

Gary spent one summer with the family of his mother's cousin. The book *Harris and Me* is based on that summer. In an online chat, Paulsen said, "It's all essentially true. I spent one summer with a cousin, and we spent the whole summer getting in trouble. He was nine and a half and I was seven or eight. I can't believe we lived through it. It was wonderful to write it. I had a grand time with that book!"[2]

In *Harris and Me*, the narrator and his cousin Harris help with the farm chores, hide from a mean, sneaky rooster, and ride enormous horses. They also find plenty of ways to get into trouble. While pretending to fight in a war, they leap into a

> **"I had a really rough childhood. Both my parents were drunks and just hated each other. . . . to me childhood was mainly something to get through alive."**
>
> **—Gary Paulsen**

pig pen, startle the pigs, and get trampled in the mud. After reading Tarzan comic books, they try to swing through the barnyard on a rope without touching the ground. Inspired by a cowboy movie, they plan to jump from the hayloft onto a horse's back. By the end of the summer, the narrator feels he belongs on the farm. He does not want to go back home.

As Gary grew older, he felt that way himself

more and more. As he wrote later, "I had a really rough childhood. Both my parents were drunks and just hated each other. They fought and screamed and never should have been married. I can remember hiding under the kitchen table and just wishing they were gone. So to me childhood was mainly something to get through alive."[3] He had to do much of his growing up alone. As he later explained, "I learned to iron clothes at seven and fed myself for years."[4]

Gary's family moved from the failed chicken farm to Thief River Falls, Minnesota. Gary's father held—and lost—job after job. Every chance he got, Gary got away from his miserable life at home. He spent weekends hunting with relatives. He often fled to the woods on his own. "In those days," he said, "there were no programs to help, no government agencies, but the problems were still there; the abuse and alcohol and emotional strain and pain—all existed then and before then, except that when a young person had trouble, there wasn't any way to fix it. The young would either have to stand and take it, which many did, to great and lasting harm, or they could cut and run. I ran to the woods and rivers of northern Minnesota."[5]

To escape from his parents, he also spent time in the basement of his family's apartment building. "I had found a place in back of the furnace, a sort of alcove, with a half-sized couch and a light hanging from the ceiling. That became my home. I'd usually take down a quart of milk and would eat grape jelly and peanut butter sandwiches down there. I made a lot of airplane models. And I slept there at night. Or I would take off for a week and go stay with an uncle to work on his farm or to go hunting. Half the time my parents wouldn't know I was gone."[6]

When Gary was twelve, his uncle gave him a rifle. He began hunting rabbits and ruffed grouse after school and on weekends. He spent whole weekends alone in the woods, camping and cooking the food he shot. The next year, he started hunting ducks. He often left home at three o'clock in the morning to get to a swamp before the ducks flew in. There, he met a dog that had been trained as a retriever. The dog wore a tag that said, "My name is Ike." *My Life in Dog Years* describes how they hunted together, day after day. One day, the dog disappeared. Thirty years later, Paulsen met Ike's trainer. The man had been injured in the Korean War and was unable to hunt when he returned. After that, his dog stayed by his side.

Gary's family kept moving, and Gary changed schools many times. He often spent only a few months in one place before leaving again. "School, to me, was just a place where I didn't fit," he said. "I didn't have the right hair, I thought my clothes were ugly, I never had many friends, I couldn't talk to girls, and the classes . . . the classes were nightmares to me. The concept that people were there to help me learn—I just didn't get that, any of that, and I wish I had. I tried to be invisible, and I never paid much attention in class, just enough to get by."[7] His grades were poor, and he skipped school often. He barely passed ninth grade because he missed so many classes.

That year, Gary decided to try to impress his classmates. He tracked a deer for two days and a night. He followed it through the woods until it could not keep going, and then he touched it. After all that effort, no one believed him and he still suffered at school. *Tracker*, the story of a boy who follows a deer while thinking of his ailing grandfather, is based on that childhood experience.

In *Tracker*, John Borne, who is thirteen and lives with his grandparents, hunts alone for the first time. The family needs meat for the winter, but the deer he follows is different from any other he has seen before. "She stood and stared at him for what seemed like hours, stood with little puffs of steam coming out of her nostrils in the moonlight, flaring to smell him, and didn't run. . . . She left something in John, a picture of beauty that hung in his mind the way a picture will sometimes stay in your eyes when you close them, burned in."[8] He follows her tracks through the snow, catching up to her from time to time. Each time, he has to decide whether to shoot the deer or let it live.

Like John Borne, Gary found comfort in the woods. "I have since come to believe that my true classroom was in the wilds and between the pages of books," he said.[9]

To earn money for food, clothes, and school supplies, Gary took jobs wherever he could. During the summer he worked on farms. During the school year he worked in a bowling alley, setting up the bowling pins after they were knocked down. Some nights, he worked for four hours and earned only a dollar. To make more money, Gary also sold newspapers in bars, often staying out until midnight.

Late at night, he often ran into groups of boys who surrounded him and stole his money. One night, he left the bowling alley carrying a hamburger to eat at home. He crawled out on the roof to try to avoid the other boys. As he stepped off the fire escape, he heard a dog growl. He gave the dog half of his hamburger and ran—right into the boys who had been tormenting him. The leader, nicknamed Happy, was "built like an upright freezer and had just about half the intelligence." Gary expected to be beaten up again, but the dog appeared, chased the boys off, and followed him home.

Gary named the dog Dirk. In the basement, he fed Dirk crackers and fell asleep. The next morning, Dirk followed Gary to school, waited for him outside, and then followed him to the bowling alley. On the way there, they met the same boys again, and one of them aimed a punch at Gary. Dirk bit the boy and chased him away. From then on, the boys stayed out of Gary's way. Dirk's story is also included in *My Life in Dog Years*.

One cold winter night as he waited to sell newspapers, Gary passed the library. He had never been inside before, but it looked inviting, so he decided to stop in to warm up. The librarian

Gary Paulsen's love of books began when he entered a library to escape the harsh Minnesota snow and cold.

offered him a library card. His whole life changed at that moment. "I was suddenly and completely overwhelmed," he wrote later. "Nobody had ever given me anything. I fought every night to keep my paper money away from the bigger street boys, had learned to hide and cheat and deal and steal, and here, with no hidden reason, this woman had given me a card."

Gary became a reader from that point on. He borrowed books from the library, read them at home in the basement, and returned for more. "The second book led to another and another and another still," he said. "Month after month, while my life didn't change and my parents kept drinking and I hustled newspapers in bars and set pins in the bowling alley and failed in school, a year when everything else fell apart, she smiled at me and gave me books."[10]

The librarian handed Gary adventure stories, Westerns, and mysteries. She introduced him to science fiction and the classics. For the boy with the troubled family life, reading became another form of escape. "I roared through everything she gave me. It was as though I had been dying of thirst and the librarian handed me a five-gallon bucket of water," he said.[11] "I have been lucky at it and

> "It was as though I had been dying of thirst and the librarian handed me a five-gallon bucket of water."
>
> —Gary Paulsen

have published many books and have won some awards and made some money and gained some recognition and run the Iditarod and sailed boats on the sea and ridden horses in the mountains, and I continue to have a good life. And all of it, every single bit of it, goes back to that one cold night and the librarian with the glasses sliding down her nose who saw more in me than I saw in myself."[12] He never learned the woman's name.

At one point, Gary landed in the care of a "big, dumb rednecked cop" who watched over him for two years. They became friends after the officer caught Gary trying to break into a garage to steal some skis. "Every night at eight o'clock he'd run watch," Paulsen wrote later. "I'd move in the back of the patrol car, and I'd sleep from eight to four in the morning while he drove around, and then we'd go hunting."[13] His book *Winterkill* is based on that friendship.

When Gary was fifteen, he ran away from home. Paulsen wrote about this period of his life in two books, *Tiltawhirl John*, published in 1977, and *The Beet Fields: Memories of a Sixteenth Summer*, published in 2000.

Tiltawhirl John is fiction—a story based on Paulsen's experiences. In an Author's Note in *The Beet Fields*, he explained, "I have been telling stories for many years, mining my life for the ore that makes each piece of fiction, as most writers mine their lives for material to make stories come to life and dance. Because of that, small portions of this book appeared in softer forms, shadowed and sketched and changed into gentler fiction, over twenty years ago. But here it is now, as real as I can write it, and as real as I can remember it happening."[14]

In both books, a fifteen-year-old boy runs away from home and hitchhikes to find work. In both books, the boy works on sugar beet farms in North Dakota, thinning the plants with a hoe. The narrator in *Tiltawhirl John* describes the job. "Hoeing sugar beets is the most boring work in the whole world. It's worse than watching grass grow—so stupid and dumb and boring that pretty soon you forget what you're doing, and the work takes over and your mind goes away while you chop without thinking. You get into this rhythm where you hoe and step, and hoe and step, and it doesn't take long before you don't even see the beets anymore. Your eyes glaze over and the sun cooks you and it's like you've never done anything else in your life but hoe beets, never been anywhere but in the beet fields."[15]

In both books, the boy works with a group of Mexican laborers who entered the country illegally to find work. In *Tiltawhirl John*, the boy escapes after a fight with the farmer. In *The Beet Fields*, the boy stays on one farm to work after the beets have been picked. Day after day, he drives a tractor from dawn to dusk, drinking coffee to stay awake. He escapes from a sheriff who suspects he is a runaway.

In both books, the boy joins a group of carnival workers. In both books, the boy learns lessons

Gary Paulsen wrote two different books capturing his experiences farming sugar beets (above).

about greed, pride, trust, and respect. In *The Beet Fields*, Paulsen writes, "In the first week with the carnival the boy learned more than he had in his whole life before that, and in some ways more than he would learn in all the time he lived afterward. He learned carny rules, carny thoughts, carny lives. He learned that everybody who wasn't with the carnival and some who were with the carnival were suckers."[16]

Eventually, the boy in each book learns to trust his own judgment. As the narrator says in *Tiltawhirl John*, "Because in the end it's like T-John said once: some people like thunder and some like the rain. And not everybody likes the thunder and not everybody likes the rain. Going off to seek my fame and fortune was maybe like tasting the thunder, even though I'm a person who likes rain best."[17]

Gary graduated from high school in 1957 in Thief River Falls, Minnesota, with low grades. "I squeezed through with Cs and Ds," he said.[18] He did not know what to do next.

CHAPTER 4

Finding Himself

After he finished high school, Gary Paulsen registered for college in Bemidji, Minnesota. He planned to study engineering. He paid the tuition with money he earned by trapping animals for the state. His college grades were poor, and he left after only one year.

In 1959, when he was nineteen, Paulsen joined the army. In the army, he studied electrical engineering and missile technology. He spent time at army bases in Colorado, Oklahoma, and Texas. He hated army life, and he later wrote, "I enlisted in the army—only a little drunk—and got to spend three years, eight months, twenty-one days, and nine hours regretting it."[1] By the time he left in 1962, he had become a sergeant.

After Paulsen left the army, he studied engineering. He became an electronics engineer in the aerospace industry. "I worked on the Gemini shots, the Mariner probes and on designing the guidance section for the Shrike, an anti-radar missile," he said. "I was good at my work, but I didn't like it."[2]

Paulsen got married, and he and his wife had two children, Lance and Lynn. In 1965, at 26, he was working at the Goldstone Deep Space Tracking Center, a satellite tracking station in California. One night, he read a magazine article about flight-testing a new airplane. All of a sudden, he knew what he wanted to do.

"I was tracking satellites one night when I had an epiphany and realized I needed to be a writer," he said. "I had never thought of writing before then. I didn't even know what a manuscript was. But it was an absolute dead-bang certainty."[3] In a matter of hours, he figured out how to change careers. He left his job that night. He decided to find a job editing a magazine.

Paulsen filled a resume with impressive—but false—work experience. With his fake resume, he found a job in Hollywood as an associate editor at a company that published about twenty men's magazines. His employers soon realized that he had more ambition than experience. Luckily for him, they taught him how to do the work. Paulsen spent nearly a year working for the company. That work taught him more about writing than anything else he had ever done. "It was very good training," he said. "Editing taught me to get to the point with words. And it taught me that writing isn't about ego but about getting the words right."[4]

During the day, Paulsen proofread magazines about American history, plumbing, and paint. He worked on articles about motorcycles, farming, and coffins. He learned how to write copy and design photo spreads for the magazines. At night, he wrote. His coworkers read his work and told him what they thought of it. After almost a year of working this way, he sold his first article.

While he lived in California, Paulsen also worked as an extra in movies. He taught himself sculpture, mostly wood-carving, and once won

> **"Editing taught me to get to the point with words. And it taught me that writing isn't about ego but about getting the words right."**
>
> **—Gary Paulsen**

first prize in an art exhibition in Santa Barbara. He and his first wife divorced, and he remarried.

Paulsen soon realized he did not belong in Hollywood. In 1966, he moved back to Minnesota with his second wife. There, he kept working on his writing. To survive, he snared rabbits and speared northerns through the ice. Finally, he started selling books.

His first book, *The Special War*, was an adult book about Vietnam. *Some Birds Don't Fly*, his next book, was a nonfiction book for adults that Paulsen said was awful. Soon after that, he finished *Mr. Tucket*, a work of historical fiction about a boy traveling with a wagon train. He also wrote magazine articles.

At this time, Paulsen felt success was right around the corner. He bought a sailboat in California and lived on it for about six months. In 1967, he moved to an artists' colony in Taos, New Mexico, planning to write. Instead, he started drinking. He found he could not focus on his writing when he drank, so he worked in construction jobs instead.

One good thing happened in Taos. A few months after he moved there, he met his third wife, the painter Ruth Ellen Wright. One day, as his second marriage was ending, he waited in a post office. Ruth stood behind him in line. FBI agents appeared, searching for someone, and Paulsen was worried. For some reason, the FBI had been interested in one of his books. He turned to Ruth and asked her to hold his money for him. As soon as he saw her eyes, he fell in love. They got to know each other after the agents left. They moved to Colorado in 1969 and were married in 1971. Later that year, their son Jim was born.

Paulsen battled alcoholism for several years. During a trip back to Taos to visit old friends, he realized that his problem with alcohol was destroying his life. He finally quit drinking for good on his second wedding anniversary. "Alcohol took over my life," he said, "but I quit in 1973."

While still in Colorado, Paulsen began writing again. After two years, he sold an adult nonfiction book about building and remodeling a home. Over the next few years, he wrote several adult mysteries and two more books about home repairs. He wrote a series of sports books for young adults. Then he signed a contract with a new publishing company. He borrowed money, expecting to pay it back with the money he earned from the contract, but the company did not pay him for the books he wrote. With some cash he had set aside, he drove back to Minnesota in 1979 with his wife and son. He bought twelve acres of land near Bemidji, and the family spent the winter there with no plumbing or electricity. Paulsen trapped game for food.

Around this time, Paulsen also fought a legal battle. His book *Winterkill* is the story of a boy from an abusive family who is guided by a police officer. After it was published, someone he had known in Minnesota sued him for libel. The book's publisher left him to defend himself. After taking the case all the way to the state Supreme Court, Paulsen eventually won. But the experience left him angry and almost bankrupt. At that point, he was so upset that he quit writing for a while.

In his book *Woodsong*, Paulsen describes what happened next. "The state of Minnesota was having a rough time with beavers. They had more or less run amuck and were damming up rivers and flooding highways, filling pastures, even beginning to invade the cities. I had trapped a bit when I was a boy, and to make some money I decided to trap for the state—the state paid a small bounty and the pelt brought a similar small amount of money." Paulsen set up a twenty-mile line of animal traps. He traveled along the trapline on foot or on skis. Then one day, a friend gave him a broken dogsled and four older dogs—Storm, Yogi, Obeah, and Columbia.

Paulsen fixed the sled and started learning how to run the dogs. He added three more dogs to his team and extended the trapline to almost sixty miles. At first, he ran the dogs to check the traps during the day. At night, he set up a tent, unrolled his sleeping bag, and slept with the dogs. Later, he learned that dogs run better at night.

Over time, Paulsen gained so much respect for the dogs and for other animals, that he decided he could not trap anymore. He realized it was wrong for him to kill, but he kept running the dogs anyway. In spite of bitter cold and serious injuries, he ran thousands of miles on his dogsled.

People who travel over snow by dogsled are called mushers. "Mush" is the command they give the dogs to make them start running. The term comes from the French word for "march."

Two of Paulsen's other books for younger and older audiences tell similar stories about mushing. *Dogteam* is a picture book illustrated by his wife, Ruth Wright Paulsen. In it, Paulsen's poetic text describes the dogs dancing "through the trees, in and out, the sled whipping after them through the trees with no sound but the song of the runners, the high-soft-shusshh-whine of the runners and

Gary Paulsen is pulled along by his dogsled team in February 2005.

the soft jingle of their collars." In an endnote, he says, "Nothing in running dogs is quite so beautiful as a night run—the cold is crisper, the dogs run for the pure joy of running, and the moon seems to dance on the snow. In all of our running and training and raising puppies the night runs stand out the most."[5]

With his love for dogs and for running with them, it is not surprising that Paulsen turned to

> "Nothing in running dogs is quite so beautiful as a night run—the cold is crisper, the dogs run for the pure joy of running, and the moon seems to dance on the snow."
>
> —Gary Paulsen

dogsled racing. In 1983, he entered the Iditarod, a grueling dogsled race across Alaska from Anchorage to Nome. The race is expensive, and Paulsen was not rich. He had well-trained dogs, but he needed enough money to move them and all his supplies to Alaska. With all the time he spent training, he had no time left to work.

By that time, Paulsen had already written more than forty books. Besides his novels, he had written a biography, a book about careers, and a couple of nonfiction books about animals. A few of his adult books described how to build and remodel homes. A series of sports books for kids had titles such as *Running, Jumping, and Throwing—If You Can*; *Tackling, Running, and Kicking—Now and Again*; and *Facing Off, Checking, and Goaltending—Perhaps*.

As Paulsen was preparing for the race he heard from Richard Jackson, an editor who then worked at Bradbury Press. Jackson had read some of Paulsen's work, and he asked Paulsen to write for him. Paulsen said he was too busy training to write. Jackson sent Paulsen some money to help cover his race expenses. He asked Paulsen to submit the next book he wrote. They became a team.

Winterdance: The Fine Madness of Running the Iditarod is an adult book that describes Paulsen's experiences the first time he ran the 1,180-mile race.

To prepare for the race, Paulsen had to put together a team of reliable dogs. He and Ruth drove to Canada to pick up three dogs that fought in the back of the truck all the way home. Paulsen called them "huge, gray-sided, yellow-eyed meat eaters that didn't want anything but to pull and eat; no petting, no love, no hate, no touch. Just a harness and a horizon."[6]

Besides the dogs, he needed something for them to pull. First, he hooked five dogs to an old bicycle he had bought at a rummage sale. He climbed on the bike, and the dogs took off. When a rabbit crossed their path, the dogs chased after it. Paulsen was able to hold on until a tree limb knocked him off the bike. The dogs kept going.

He followed them for miles before he caught up with them back at home.

Next, he tried building a light training rig on wheelbarrow wheels. He welded pipes together to make the frame. He kept adding dogs to his team. One day, he hooked up thirteen dogs. As the dogs tore out of the yard, the rig overturned. All the gear flew off, and Paulsen was dragged along the road. He finally righted the broken rig and mushed thirty miles in less than three hours.

Finally, he hooked the dogs up to an old car. For the first run, he took the dogs out at night, and they kept running into skunks. By the time they got home, Paulsen smelled so bad that he slept in the kennel with the dogs. That experience changed the way he and the dogs thought of each other. Even the most difficult dogs began to accept him, and he realized he had a lot to learn from the dogs.

"Dogs are almost a religion to me," Paulsen once said. "They are the best thing that ever happened to the human race. Here is an animal that just loves. It doesn't give a darn who you are or what you are. It doesn't care if you're rich, if you're poor, if you're ugly. They just worship you and will do anything for you. They will lay down their lives for you."[7]

CHAPTER 5

Good News and Bad

In a dogsled race, caring for the dogs is the most important task. For the Iditarod, a team can include from seven to twenty dogs. They all eat a snack every hour and a full meal every four hours. They wear booties to protect their feet in the snow and ice. Their feet must be checked often for injury. Between runs, they need to rest.

Eighteen checkpoints are set up along the route. All the mushers' food and supplies must be flown there ahead of the race. If the sled or the harnesses are damaged along the way, the musher must stop and make repairs.

On his sled, Paulsen carried extra food for the dogs and himself. He packed headlamp batteries, extra harness line, spare clothes, a portable stove, a thermos, and safety equipment. He also brought a portable tape player with a Willie Nelson tape.

At the start of the race, Paulsen's lead dog missed a turn. Instead of leaving Anchorage, he led the team right through town. "We went through people's yards, ripped down fences, knocked over garbage cans," Paulsen wrote. "I heard later that at the banquet some people had been speaking of me and I was unofficially voted the least likely to get out of Anchorage."[1] Finally, he took the snowhook, an anchor that keeps the dogs from running off when the sled is stopped. He used it to catch a stop sign and regain control of the team. He switched the dogs' places and put in a new leader. Then he had to ask for directions to get back to the course.

The rest of the race was not much easier. *Winterdance* describes the challenges of the course. Along the way, Paulsen faced a moose attack, another wrong turn, snowstorms, and several dogfights. Those troubles took place in subzero temperatures while he suffered from a serious lack of sleep.

Dogsleds can only move about ten miles per hour in good conditions. Deep snow can slow them down to two or three miles per hour. Paulsen reached Nome and finished the race in seventeen days and twelve hours. Of the seventy-three mushers, he came in forty-second—an amazing feat for a first attempt. As he wrote later, "there's a point where you are alone with your dogs in the vastness of the Alaska Range, you and the dogs and the peaks—you know you will never be the same again."[2]

After the 1983 Iditarod, Paulsen wrote *Dogsong*, the story of a boy from a small Eskimo village who wants to learn the old ways of his people. Russel Susskit moves in with an old man named Oogruk. He learns how to run Oogruk's dogs and takes them on a long journey north. He learns how to hunt and how to survive in the wilderness.

> ## "[T]here's a point where you are alone with your dogs in the vastness of the Alaska Range, you and the dogs and the peaks—you know you will never be the same again."
>
> **—Gary Paulsen**

The book was inspired by a boy Paulsen met during the race. Paulsen had arrived in a village at midnight. The boy ran up to Paulsen and asked him to bring the team to his house so he could learn about dogs and sleds. The dogs were fighting, and Paulsen was afraid the boy would be hurt. He later realized the boy was trying to find his heritage. "I am stunned that an Eskimo boy on the Bering Sea would have to ask someone from Minnesota about dogs," he said.[3]

Dogsong was published in 1985. It was the third book Richard Jackson edited, after *Dancing*

How the Iditarod Began

In January 1925, the temperature in the middle of Alaska was fifty degrees below zero. Along the Bering Sea coast, winds gusted up to eighty miles per hour. In the coastal town of Nome, children were dying from diphtheria. The only medicine in Alaska was in Anchorage, more than a thousand miles away.

No airplanes were available to transport the medicine. The railroad ended at Nenana, still 674 miles from Nome. Dogsleds were the only way to get the medicine from there to the children.

The first musher left late at night on January 27. He carried the medicine, wrapped up in quilts and furs. Twenty mushers each rode about thirty miles through bitter cold and blinding snow. One musher covered 84 miles in one day! For almost 250 miles, the

Gary Paulsen prepares his dogsled team for a run near his home in Willow, Alaska, on February 10, 2005.

route followed the frozen Yukon River. The medicine arrived in Nome early on the morning of February 2, only 127 hours and 30 minutes later. The speed record stands to this day. Balto, the lead dog that made it to Nome, was featured in a movie.

The children of Nome were saved by the heroic efforts of twenty dogsled mushers and their powerful dogs. The Iditarod is held each year in memory of that life-saving run.

Carl (1983) and *Tracker* (1984). Both earlier books had gotten good reviews.

Paulsen entered the Iditarod again in 1985 but scratched when he was only eighty miles from Nome. In the middle of a blizzard, a gust of wind picked up the lead dogs and tossed them back over him and the rest of the team. Luckily, they all survived. But they had to be rescued by plane. *Guts: The True Stories Behind Hatchet and the Brian Books* includes a thrilling description of that flight. The dogs panicked and ran to the rear of the plane, and Paulsen had to keep throwing them forward to keep the plane balanced.

Even during that stormy 1985 race, he was writing, working on *Hatchet*, a survival story set in the Canadian wilderness. He wrote longhand while the dogs slept. "I've learned to map out a whole book in my head before I even start to write it," he said.[4]

In 1986, *Dogsong* won a Newbery Honor Medal. Paulsen credited Jackson's editing. "I think he's the best editor in the business," he said. "Dick Jackson helped me a lot." The award "changed everything," Paulsen said.[5]

The Newbery Medal is the oldest and best-known award for children's books. The award is given each year to the author of the "most distinguished American children's book" published during the previous year. It is awarded by the Association for Library Service to Children, a division of the American Library Association (ALA). Each year, a committee chooses one medal winner and one or more other books considered worthy of attention.

The Young Adult Library Services Association (YALSA) is a division of the ALA. YALSA compiles an annual list called Best Books for Young Adults.

> **Young readers grabbed onto the book and did not let it go. They simply could not get enough of Brian Robeson and his adventures.**

Books on the list can be fiction or nonfiction written for ages 12 to 18. They are chosen for their "proven or potential appeal to the personal reading tastes of the young adult." The ALA Notable Children's Books List is compiled by a committee of the Association for Library Service to Children (ALSC). Notable books are "worthy of note or notice, important, distinguished, outstanding."

Year after year, Paulsen's books appear on these and other lists of recommended books.

In 1988, *Hatchet* won a Newbery Honor Medal. Young readers grabbed onto the book and did not let it go. They simply could not get enough of Brian Robeson and his adventures. Paulsen spoke about the response to *Hatchet* in an interview. He said that readers love *Hatchet* and books like it because of the concept of survival. "So many of them are trying to survive in almost impossible situations—the inner city, for example. It's very difficult to get through these kinds of things. And as readers they relate to the concept of Brian surviving."[6]

That same year, *The Island* was published. The main character, Wil Neuton, is a boy whose family moves from Madison, Wisconsin, to a cabin in the north woods. He finds an island where he stays when he can, trying to understand his life and himself. The book got mixed reviews, but it did get attention.

The Winter Room, published in 1989, was Paulsen's third Newbery Honor Book. Two brothers sit with their family on winter nights and listen to their Uncle David tell stories. One night, he tells a story the boys do not believe, and it splits the family apart. An amazing event brings them back together again.

In 1990, Paulsen was training to run the Iditarod again. Two of his dogs started fighting, so he got between them. "I grabbed each of them and pulled them apart," he wrote. "They fought to get

Paulsen relaxes with Flax, his favorite husky, just outside his
Alaskan home in February 2005.

back at each other and I pulled harder and felt a sudden pain in my chest. I had once ripped my sternum loose and I thought that's what had happened.

"The pain went away, but a week later I had to fly to Boston on business and in the Boston airport for no apparent reason the same pain came back and this time I knew what it was. The tests proved positive. I had heart disease."[7]

Over the years, Gary Paulsen had held many jobs. He had worked as a teacher, an electronics field engineer, a truck driver, a trapper, and a professional archer. He was a migrant farmworker, a sailor, a farmer, a rancher. He spent time as an actor, a singer, a director, and a sculptor. But he was not prepared for the next big change in his life.

"Of course, you can't run the Iditarod again," Paulsen's doctor said. Paulsen needed medicine, exercise, and a strict diet. His hectic work schedule had to slow down. He could still live an active life. But he had to face the prospect of living without the dogs that had brought him so much joy.

Paulsen sold all but one dog—thirty of them, plus their stakes, chains, equipment, and doghouses—to another musher. The dog he kept, Cookie, had run nearly fourteen thousand miles with him. In *My Life in Dog Years*, Paulsen describes how Cookie once saved his life. On a long run along a beaver trapline, Paulsen fell through thin ice into deep water. On the way down, he grabbed a rope that was tied to the sled. Cookie's eyes locked on his.

"She saw me drop, instantly analyzed the situation, got the team up—she must have jerked them to their feet—got them pulling, and they pulled me out."[8] He started a whole tree on fire so he could warm up and dry his clothes.

Paulsen also wrote about Cookie in *Puppies, Dogs, and Blue Northers: Reflections on Being Raised by a Pack of Sled Dogs*. "We talked often," he said, "sometimes at great length; I frequently explained parts of my life to her, which sometimes helped me understand myself better, and if she didn't know all the words (actually, she did recognize many individual words) she was a master at tones. She could tell by the sound of my voice if I was happy, sad, angry, distracted, worried, unsure, positive, lying, telling the truth, if I truly believed in what I was saying or needed to be argued with to be certain. A hundred, a thousand times a year we 'negotiated' differences—when and where best to go—and almost invariably she was right."[9] For years, Paulsen carried Cookie's picture in his wallet. It was a constant reminder of the life he missed.

CHAPTER 6

Lifestyle Changes

When he found out he could not run the dogs anymore, Paulsen moved to southern New Mexico. For about a year, he and Ruth divided their time between Minnesota, New Mexico, and Wyoming.

In 1991, Paulsen received the ALAN Award from the Assembly on Literature for Adolescents of the National Council of Teachers of English (NCTE). The award honors people who have made outstanding contributions to the field of adolescent literature.

The Paulsens settled in New Mexico in 1992, and Paulsen kept writing.

"There was suddenly an eighteen-hour hole in my day," he said.[1] He poured the energy he had put into mushing into writing instead. As he put it, "I started to focus on writing the same energies and efforts that I was using with dogs. So we're talking 18-, 19-, 20-hour days completely committed to work. Totally, viciously, obsessively committed to work, the way I'd run dogs. My output dramatically increased, and there were other areas I wanted to explore. . . . I still work that way, completely, all the time. I just work. I don't drink, I don't fool around, I'm just this way. . . . The end result is there's a lot of books out there."[2]

As he increased his output, he also changed publishers. He worked with George Nicholson and David Gale at Delacorte. Not only did Paulsen

> ## "I started to focus on writing the same energies and efforts that I was using with dogs. . . . The end result is there's a lot of books out there."
>
> **—Gary Paulsen**

write a lot of books, he wrote a lot of different kinds of books. During the 1990s, he experimented with new styles of writing. "Sometimes the way to tell a story is even more important than the story itself," he said.[3]

Sisters/Hermanas, published in 1993, uses two points of view. Rosa and Traci are both fourteen years old. Traci is a wealthy American girl who has everything she ever wanted. Rosa is a Mexican girl living in the country illegally and trying to make a living on her own. In alternating chapters, their stories show the contrast between their lives. They meet in a moment of crisis. A creative book design includes both English and Spanish versions in one book.

Paulsen had used alternating points of view in earlier books. In *Canyons*, published in 1990, a boy finds a skull belonging to an Apache boy killed by soldiers more than a hundred years earlier. The first chapters include the stories of both boys. "I wanted there not to be a difference," Paulsen said. "I wanted the two boys to be the same, to have the same brain. I don't want any differences between people anymore. . . . I wanted the time to not matter and I wanted the people to not matter. I wanted them to be the same no matter what, and so that's what I did. I decided I'd take two completely opposite types of humans and they could become the same person."[4]

Sentries, published in 1986, contrasts the stories of four contemporary young people with those of three soldiers in past wars. It ends with the imaginary start of World War III. A *School Library Journal* review called the format "choppy" and said that the ending does not work within the structure of the book. On the other hand, it said, Paulsen does manage to involve readers.

The theme of war appears in several of Paulsen's works. His writing has been influenced by his experiences in the army. He knew people who fought in Korea, World War II, and Vietnam. As a boy, he saw the effects of war in the

Philippines. "It was terrible," he said. "All of those affected me."[5]

The Foxman, an antiwar novel published in 1977, was called "one of his most important and powerful books."[6] A fifteen-year-old boy and his cousin meet a man who lives alone in the woods because he was disfigured in World War I. The boy learns survival techniques from the man, who earned his name from the fox pelts hanging in his hut.

The Monument, published in 1994, is the story of an orphaned girl who is finally adopted. Rachel, or Rocky, has a bad leg and a dog named Python. She meets an artist hired by the town to design a monument to local soldiers who were killed in wars. Rocky follows the artist around town while he sketches. "If I could have wrapped the rest of that first day in plastic and kept it in a box to keep forever to take out and play with, I would have been happy," she says.

The artist teaches Rocky how to draw. "Watch and learn and work and live and be," he tells her.

About the book, Paulsen said, "I wanted to show art, show how it can shake and crumble thinking, how it can bring joy and sadness at the same time; how it can own and be owned, sweep through lives and change them—how the beauty of it . . . can grow from even that ultimate ruin of all ruins: the filth of war."[7]

In *The Car*, also published in 1994, Terry Anders builds a car from a kit to escape from his parents, who abandoned him. He leaves Cleveland

Paulsen speaks during an International Reading Association (IRA) convention in March 2006.

alone to search for an uncle in Oregon but ends up traveling with a pair of Vietnam veterans. Instead of finding his family, he forms a bond with the two trouble-prone men. A *Publishers Weekly* review said, "Besides evoking a type of independence and tough-mindedness that will appeal to teens, this provocative novel introduces and explores some interesting philosophies of life while stressing the value of learning from experience. Once again the Newbery Honor author demonstrates his abilities to create flesh-and-blood characters and to relate a message without preaching a moral."

Soldier's Heart (1998) is the story of fifteen-year-old Charley Goddard, who enlists and serves in the Civil War. "I discovered Charley Goddard when reading a book about the Minnesota First Volunteers," Paulsen said.[8] Charley was a real person who fought in several battles and was shot more than once. He survived the war but died a few years later from the trauma.

The Rifle, a 1994 book, follows the history of a gun from the time it is made in 1768. The gunsmith "was an artist, pure and simple; he was that perfect blending of artistic thinking and force of hand that it took to make a sweet rifle," one that is "a weapon of such beauty and accuracy . . . that it might be actually worshiped."[9] The gunsmith sells the rifle to a hunter for a whole year's worth of hides. The hunter joins a group of volunteers fighting for independence from the British. After he dies in the war, the rifle stays in an attic for two hundred years before it is found, sold, and sold again. After a tragic accident, the rifle changes hands again and waits for another opportunity.

About writing *The Rifle*, Paulsen said, "I wanted to show that at one time rifles and weapons were extremely important to what we are—to the country, and that has become warped—insanely warped, and now they're like a disease. Weapons are just an epidemic—kids shooting people. . . . I've never had to actually use a weapon to defend myself against a person, but I have with bear and moose, and I'm really glad I had a weapon. But they're horrible. People do not understand that firearms are not toys; they're weapons—they are for killing."[10]

Paulsen's work in those years went beyond historical fiction. He even wrote a science fiction book, *The Transall Saga*. While hiking alone, Mark Harrison falls into a strange beam of light and travels through time. He wakes up in a strange landscape with weird creatures. To survive, he must find food and build a shelter. He has to make weapons and teach himself how to hunt. Above all, he has to find his way back to the shaft of light.

In the 1990s, Ruth Wright Paulsen illustrated several of Paulsen's picture books. *The Tortilla Factory* describes how corn grows from seeds and is turned into tortillas. A review in *Booklist* called it "an interesting and attractive offering." *Canoe Days* uses poetic language to describe a quiet canoe trip on a calm summer day. In *Worksong,*

Paulsen's rhyming text shows people working at many kinds of jobs.

But Paulsen did not spend all his time writing. After he stopped running sled dogs, he rode horses. He missed the dogs terribly, and he said that spending time with horses saved him.

"Since diagnosed with heart disease I have seen cliff dwellings and deserts and mountains, have ridden with the ghosts of famous Sioux like Crazy Horse and the dead soldiers who fought

> **"They gave me a chance to see and be more at a time when many men—some of them dear and good friends of mine—simply lay down and died."**
>
> **—Gary Paulsen**

him; of Apaches and black Tenth Cavalry troopers who hunted them; have dodged bear and been hit by snakes and fallen down mountains and swum rivers and been knocked down by flash floods and seen sunsets and dawns that no man, ever, has seen before or will see again in the same way or place; have heard coyotes and chased antelope and deer and watched desert storms march across the world and lain under stars so bright and clear you could see the life in them. . . . All this was from the horses; from Merry and Blackie. They gave me a chance to see and be more at a time when many men—some of them dear and good friends of mine—simply lay down and died."[11]

As usual, Paulsen mined his own life for inspiration. Even riding horses became research for another book, *The Haymeadow*. In the book, a boy spends a summer in a Wyoming meadow. Like his father and grandfather had years earlier, he watches six thousand sheep. His only companions are four dogs and two horses. The story was inspired by a friend's childhood.

In the final chapter of *My Life in Dog Years*, Paulsen describes a trip into the Bighorn Mountains from Story, Wyoming. His dog Josh led the way. "All mountains are beautiful but there is something about the Bighorns that is particularly wonderful, and I have trained one horse to carry a pack so I can head up and spend some time alone wandering, looking."[12]

Many of Paulsen's adventures are solo ones. When he travels alone, he can pay more attention to the details of what he sees. His writing is realistic because he includes those details. He once compared this method of paying attention to acting like a wolf. "Wolves see and listen to every single thing," he said. "So I started doing that."[13]

CHAPTER 7

Sailboats, Motorcycles, and More Books

Paulsen's work in the 1990s also included several series. In 1992, the first of the Culpepper Adventures appeared. Stories about Dunc Culpepper and his best friend, Amos Binder, were published each year for the next five years. By 1997, the two pals starred in thirty different humorous adventures. They travel back in time in *Culpepper's Cannon*. They search for buried treasure in *The Case of the Dirty Bird*. In other volumes, they solve crimes, travel around the world, and meet aliens, athletes, and monsters. "The Dunc and Amos books were fun to write and were funny," Paulsen said, "but with humor the pacing is critical, and you have to pay attention to what you are doing. . . . It's hard to do comedy. It's very serious business."[1]

In 1994, the World of Adventure series appeared. The action-packed books are written for a slightly older audience. Characters get into and out of more serious trouble, using their wits, strength, and a few martial arts skills. Each volume includes survival tips. In *Captive!*, a whole class of students and their teacher are held hostage in their bus by two men who plan to ask for ransom money and a plane to get away. Then the bus breaks down. The kidnappers take four of the boys to their mountain hideaway. The boys must stick together and leave clues for rescuers to find them.

Mr. Tucket, published in 1968, is the story of a fourteen-year-old boy who is separated from his family in 1848. They are traveling in a wagon train from Missouri to Oregon. Between 1995 and 1999, four more Francis Tucket books were published. *Call Me Francis Tucket*, *Tucket's Ride*, *Tucket's Home*, and *Tucket's Gold* follow the boy and his two young companions across the west for two years.

Alida's Song, published in 1999, is a sequel to *The Cookcamp*. The narrator, who is now fourteen, spends another summer with his grandmother. This time, she is a cook for two elderly brothers. The boy is hired to help out on the farm where she works.

The Quilt, published in 2004, is Paulsen's third book about his grandmother. It recalls another visit, when he was six years old. This time, he helps with farm chores. He finds the barn a "wonderful mystery." He carries the milking stools from cow to cow. He shoos the cats away from the cows. The only child among a group of women, he tries hard to learn from their conversations. He is too young to understand much, but the women tell him stories as they work together on a quilting project.

After the phenomenal success of *Hatchet*, readers wrote to Paulsen asking for more books about Brian Robeson. Paulsen received 250 to 400 letters a day. Although he had not planned to write a sequel, Paulsen followed up with four of them. He had no problem making each new book fresh and different from the others. "Once I started writing, I didn't think in terms of the first book at all," he said. "Monet painted haystacks over and over and they're all different. It's the same with writing about an area again."[2] In addition, Brian himself changes through the course of the books.

In *The River* (1991), Brian is asked to return to the wilderness to help scientists study survival psychology. Paulsen explained, *"The River* was a direct response to readers who sent letters telling me that Brian's story wasn't done at the end of *Hatchet*. So many wanted to know what happened to Brian after the rescue that I started wondering about him myself. What if Brian went back to the woods with the knowledge he'd gained, but this time were also responsible for the life of another person?"

Brian's Winter (1996) shows what would have happened if Brian were not rescued and had to spend the winter on his own. "When I finished *The River* I thought I'd taken his story as far as it could go," Paulsen wrote. "And then the next batch of letters started showing up. Again readers wrote that there had to be more to the story, but this time, they told me Brian had been rescued in *Hatchet* too soon—before it became really hard going."

In *Brian's Return* (1999), Brian realizes he needs to go back to the wilderness. Paulsen wrote of it, "This last book perhaps shows Brian most completely, most truly: how he is changed mentally, how he deals with home life and finally, how he must return to the woods that make him whole."[3]

> ". . . I could not shake them until I tried to figure out on paper what their lives must have been like."
>
> —Gary Paulsen

In *Brian's Hunt* (2003), Brian rescues a wounded dog and goes to search for the friends he made on his previous trip to the wilderness. Each new Brian book has brought more readers to the rest of the books.

Nightjohn, published in 1993, is the story of a slave who teaches other slaves to read, including a girl named Sarny. Paulsen said *Nightjohn* was "the result of studying history. Sarny came from the research I did in the National Archives when I

Gary Paulsen signs a copy of one of his books for a fan.

stumbled across the Slave Narratives. . . . I hadn't expected to find characters for books of my own when I started reading, but I could not shake them until I tried to figure out on paper what their lives must have been like."[4]

Paulsen continues Sarny's story in the 1997 book *Sarny: A Life Remembered*. Her story continues through the Civil War and after. When she becomes a free woman, she travels to New Orleans in search of her children. All her life, she teaches others to read. "It's all true," Paulsen said. "Not true for one person, but everything in the book happened to people. I didn't intend to write a sequel, because I was afraid it might dilute the power of the first story, but I got so many letters asking me to keep writing."[5]

In his fifties and sixties, Paulsen took several long sailboat voyages alone. In 1994, he set off to sail on the Pacific Ocean. The weather did not cooperate. Instead, he sailed from California to Mexico and back again on an old sailboat, *Felicity*, that he fixed up himself. Then he sailed north along the West Coast all the way to Alaska. He watched humpback whales that came so close to the boat he could have touched them. Killer whales fought and played nearby. After he sailed back, he took his catamaran, *Ariel*, to Hawaii, Samoa, Tonga, and Fiji. On the way back, he stopped in Hawaii and California before sailing on to the Sea of Cortez, between Mexico and the Baja peninsula.

In *Pilgrimage on a Steel Ride: A Memoir About Men and Motorcycles*, he wrote, "I was fixing up my old sailboat after coming back from Mexico and the Sea of Cortez to go across the Pacific and back around Cape Horn—where I think it is possible to look for the next grail—and I was alone and my fifty-seventh birthday came upon me."[6] That is when he decided to write about motorcycles.

Paulsen describes the bikes he has ridden. At age sixteen, he rode a Whizzer to work at a frozen vegetable factory. He owned a classic English Triumph and a dirt bike that he took on camping trips. At fifty-six, he bought a Harley-Davidson. The first time he rode it, he felt everything change. "The bike held me like a hand," he writes, "caught me and took me with it so that the engine seemed to be my engine, the wheels my wheels. . . . In some way it brought me out of myself, out ahead of myself, into myself, into the core of what I was, what I needed to live."[7] On his first trip with the bike, he rode seven hundred miles. To learn about riding, he knew he had to keep going. He had learned that from running dogs. As usual, he was mostly on his own.

"It is perhaps one of the core beauties of riding—the enforced solitude."

—Gary Paulsen

"You are always alone when you ride," he writes. "Even in a group you are alone. It is perhaps one of the core beauties of riding—the enforced solitude. With the pipes rapping and the wind screaming—the constant hurricane—even with a passenger on the back you are alone. The bike demands it, demands that you keep your attention on it, and the noise of the motor and wind keeps your thoughts internal. The only time I have ever been more alone with my thoughts is sailing alone on the Pacific and in both cases there is an elegance to the solitude, a grace that turns the act of thinking almost into a dance."[8]

To really get to know the bike, he decided to ride to Alaska. He and a companion rode through terrible rains in the Midwest and cold weather in North Dakota. At night, they stayed in motels, and Paulsen worked on *Winterdance*. In Canada, he hit a seagull and tipped over in the mud. He bounced through massive dips in the highway caused by freezing and thawing ground. When they reached Fairbanks, they turned around and rode back home.

Chapter 8

"I Never Should Have Left Dogs"

In 1997, Paulsen won the Margaret A. Edwards Award. The award honors an author's lifetime contributions in writing books for teenagers. The Young Adult Library Services Association, a division of ALA, administers the award. *School Library Journal* sponsors it. Six books were named as examples of different aspects of Paulsen's work: *Dancing Carl, Hatchet, The Crossing, The Winter Room, Woodsong,* and *Canyons.* The committee chair, Helen Vandersluis, said, "With his intense love of the outdoors and crazy courage born of adversity, Paulsen has reached young adults everywhere. His writing conveys a profound respect for their intelligence and ability to overcome life's worst realities."[1]

Paulsen uses humor as one way to make those difficult realities bearable. *The Boy Who Owned the School: A Comedy of Love*, published in 1990, is a funny story about a boy who tries to stay out of the limelight. His luck changes when the most beautiful girl in the school notices him anyway. A *Publishers Weekly* review said readers "will relish the sharp wit and incredible energy of this ironic glimpse of high school life and young romance."

The Schernoff Discoveries is the story of two social misfits who survive junior high together. They take a home economics class so they can get to know girls. They save their money to buy a car that does not work. They take revenge on football players for their constant torment. In spite of the boys' bleak situation, the book maintains a humorous tone.

Characters in other funny Paulsen books such as *Harris and Me* and *Molly McGinty Has a Really Good Day* also face their problems with wit and courage. Readers can identify with the struggles of these underdogs.

Paulsen's writing is so believable because he has been in that position himself. "Because I was pretty much on my own by the age of seven or eight, I learned about tenacity and independence and the willingness to fight," he said. "And I can go back now to some of the things that happened to me and write about them."[2]

Some of his writing brings up painful memories. "It's always difficult for me to go back to my childhood and remember what it was like. But I wish that someone, anyone, one person, would have told me . . . that things can change, that you are not defined by who you were as a kid, that you will move beyond a crummy childhood to make a happy and productive life."[3] Perhaps one thing that makes his books so popular is that his message comes through. He cares about his readers. "I know if there is any hope at all for the human race, it has to come from young people," Paulsen said.[4]

Young readers respond to that hope. They have voted Paulsen's books favorites over and over. Paulsen's books have won many other awards and honors from publishing industry magazines, teachers' organizations, and parents' groups. His books are popular with librarians and teachers as well as children and young adults. Many are used in classrooms.

Some are adopted by whole cities in reading programs. In 2002, people in Minneapolis and St. Paul, Minnesota, read *Hatchet* as part of a citywide celebration of reading intended to bring adult and young adult readers together. The same year, the Chicago suburb of Naperville, Illinois, held a reading campaign. Naperville residents read more than 27,000 Gary Paulsen books!

Paulsen has been described as muscular and determined. For years now, he has watched his diet. He does not travel as much as he used to. Since that scary news about his heart, his health has improved.

In 2003, Paulsen was asked to appear at Ikidarod, an annual event organized by Shriners Hospitals for Children in Spokane, Washington.

Mushers from all over the country take patients for sled rides through a nearby tree farm. Paulsen was there to talk with the young patients and sign autographs.

After the event, one of the organizers asked him if he wanted to take a sled out for a ride. He borrowed the team and took off—for thirty or forty miles. That invitation brought him back to mushing.

The next year, with his heart problems under control, he bought a house with a dog kennel in Alaska. He started gathering dogs and made plans to go back there and train them.

Paulsen signed up for the 2005 Iditarod. A month before the race, he was still trying to put together a team and find time to train. His dogs had run only about six hundred miles. Most teams plan to have more than three times that amount by the date of the race. With too many commitments to agents, publishers, and researchers, Paulsen had trouble getting in enough good miles. He decided to withdraw. Encounters with moose also played a part in his decision.

In 2006, Paulsen signed up again. At 66, he was the oldest musher in the race. He is quoted in the Iditarod 2006 Media Guide: "I have come back to the Iditarod because I never should have left dogs—all the time sailing the Pacific, not a day went by that I didn't miss dogs and the dance that running them is for me. I will not leave them again."

Paulsen started the 2006 race with sixteen dogs. He was injured while making a difficult turn

Gary Paulsen with his agent, Jennifer Flannery.

through a gate. After mushing 149 miles, he was forced to scratch at Skwentna on the third morning. He was in sixty-second place at the time. His agent, Jennifer Flannery, said he was in fine spirits anyway: "I don't think finishing the race was an essential component to his happiness; he just wants to be with the dogs."[5] Paulsen stayed in Alaska to help out with the race and take notes. No doubt, he will keep writing about it.

"Writing is so much a part of the way I live that I would be lost without the discipline and routine," he said. "I write every day—every day—and it gives me balance and focus. Every day I wake up, usually at 4:30 A.M., with the sole purpose of sitting down to write with a cup of hot tea and a computer or a laptop or a pad of paper—it doesn't matter. I've written whole books in my office, in a dog kennel with a headlamp, on more airplanes than I can remember, on the trampoline of my catamaran off the shores of Fiji—it never matters where I write, just where the writing takes me."[6]

Paulsen spoke of his other interests—running sled dogs, sailing, and motorcycle and horseback riding. "I'm a writer who does those things. I don't do them to write about them. I love writing the way you fall in love. I can't NOT write. I'll never retire. When a story works, I quicken, the hair goes up on the back of my neck. Those other things just don't do it. I have 27,000 miles behind dogs. I've been across the Pacific twice, but writing is everything there is."[7]

Paulsen is still happily married to Ruth. His children are all grown now. Lance owns a construction firm, and Lynn and Jim are both teachers. Jim is also a writer.

Paulsen has written a number of books for adults, but he prefers to write for younger readers. "I think it's artistically fruitless to write for adults," he said. "Adults are locked into their lives—divorces and car payments and jobs, and they are not open or receptive to new ideas the way young people are. If you really want to write artistically, you have to write for the eighth or ninth grade. Adults just don't have time to appreciate artistic, new things."[8]

To those who want to be writers, he says, "You have to read, and I mean three books a day. Read them all. Reading is the thing that will teach you."[9]

> **"Reading is the thing that will teach you."**
>
> **—Gary Paulsen**

Paulsen still studies writing. He reads to see how other writers use language. His work has been compared to Ernest Hemingway's, but he has his own style. He writes in fragments and short sentences, and he often uses repetition to make a point.

Paulsen has a gift for turning his own life into story after story. He can look at the same experience from different angles and turn each one into a new tale. His memories provide an endless supply of inspiration.

"I don't think of myself as a famous author," he said. "I've been lucky. I don't think I've changed. I keep waiting for next week when I'll have to hoe sugar beets again. Fame has never really impressed me with its permanency. You must write. The main thing is to just keep writing. That's the important thing."[10]

Paulsen's focus, long days, and hard work pay off. These days, he works with editor Wendy Lamb, and new books keep pouring out. Three more are in the works. *The Amazing Life of Birds: The Twenty-Day Puberty Journal of Duane Homer Leech* is the humorous story of a twelve-year-old boy struggling to grow up. *Bass Reeves: The Historical Account of the Most Valiant Marshall of the Old West* is the story of a black man who was born a slave. When he is freed, he becomes a U.S. Marshall. Next in store is *The Man With the Iron Head*. As usual, Paulsen is working on three more at the same time.

How does he manage his amazing output? He might think about a book for years before he does any writing. As he writes one book, he might be researching two or three others. Somehow, he keeps all those stories straight in his head. Eager readers look forward to every single one.

In His Own Words

Author's Note: Gary Paulsen answered these questions by e-mail shortly after the 2006 Iditarod dogsled race.

JEM: *I understand you are preparing to run the Iditarod, which is a huge undertaking. Can you describe some of your preparations? How many dogs are you training? How many will you race? Are you taking part in other races to prepare?*

GP: Preparing for the Iditarod has taken years; finding the right place to live and train, searching for handlers, looking for the right dogs, living with and getting to know each dog, letting them get to know and trust me. I have 32 dogs. You have to have 16 dogs to start the race so that's how many I brought with me to Nome earlier this month. I didn't do any other races, just training runs.

JEM: *Do you still find time to write while you are preparing?*

GP: I write every day of my life no matter what I'm doing; I just use notebooks and pens when

I'm with the dogs rather than laptops or computers because it's more portable that way.

JEM: *Your Iditarod biography says that you missed dogs while you were away and you won't leave them again. Will you write more about dogs and sleds?*

GP: I will have dogs until the day I die and I will write more about them for the rest of my life. They're my life, dogs and books.

JEM: *Do you ever think about writing while you are out with the dogs, or are you completely focused on running with them?*

GP: When the dogs are running or resting, I'm writing in my head, thinking about books and kicking over ideas.

JEM: *How are your preparations for this Iditarod different from the previous two?*

GP: I don't think it's much different from the last two; maybe I'm happier to be with the dogs this time because I'd been away from them for so long.

JEM: *Do you plan to enter any more dogsled races? What other adventures lie ahead for you?*

GP: I will run dogs for the rest of my life, probably, but I don't think in terms of races. I'll be with dogs, and I'll write books and I'm not at all convinced that I'm done with the sea yet.

JEM: *You live an exciting life, and you seem to have an endless supply of ideas to write about. How do you decide what would make a good topic for a book?*

GP: I write about what I live or perhaps what other people have lived, like *Nightjohn*.

JEM: *Many of your books are based on incidents from your own life. How do you distance yourself from reality to turn it into fiction?*

GP: I don't know that distance is the best way to write, at least not for me. I try to keep myself as close as possible to the book; it's better storytelling that way, I think.

JEM: *How much of your time do you spend writing? How do you find a balance between writing and your other obligations?*

GP: I write all the time, every day, and I don't think that makes me a particularly well-balanced person.

JEM: *What work are you most proud of?*

GP: I'm always proudest of the book that I'm just starting.

JEM: *What new work are you looking forward to?*

GP: I have lists and lists of book ideas that I want to get to and they all excite me.

JEM: *If you could write only one more book, what would it be?*

GP: I'd write about dogs. Again. Still. Always.

JEM: *For years, you've been encouraging kids to read. Why is reading so important to you?*

GP: Reading saved my life when I was a kid, it really did. I think it has that potential for everyone.

JEM: *How many of your books have been made into movies? Are you pleased with the results?*

GP: I don't even remember; the best thing to do, Hemingway said, if you're letting Hollywood turn your movie into a book is throw them the book and catch the money they throw back at you. They're my books; the movies belong to someone else.

JEM: *Is there anything else you want your readers to know?*

GP: I'd want readers to know how touched I am that they read my books, that they write to me and tell me what they think. We have a great relationship and I wish I could tell them all what it means to me and how they inspire me. Each of the *Hatchet* sequels I wrote because they were asked for.

Chronology

1939   Born in Minnesota, May 17.

1946   Moved to Philippine Islands.

1949   Returned to United States.

1957   Graduated from high school.

1959   Joined the army.

1962   Left the army.

1965   Decided to become a writer.

1966   Moved to Minnesota from Hollywood with second wife; first book, *The Special War*, published.

1969   Moved to Colorado with Ruth Ellen Wright.

1971   Married Ruth Ellen Wright; later that year, son Jim was born.

1973   Stopped drinking.

1979   Moved back to Minnesota with wife and son; began mushing.

1983   First Iditarod.

1985   Second Iditarod (scratched).

1986   *Dogsong* won a Newbery Honor Medal.

1988   *Hatchet* won a Newbery Honor Medal.

1990   *The Winter Room* won a Newbery Honor Medal; diagnosed with heart disease.

1992   Moved to New Mexico.

1994   Set off to sail on the Pacific Ocean.

1995 Bought a Harley-Davidson motorcycle.

1997 Won Margaret A. Edwards Award.

2003 Appeared at Ikidarod and rode on dogsled.

2005 Signed up for Iditarod but did not start.

2006 Started Iditarod but scratched after 149 miles.

Chapter Notes

Chapter 1. "You Use What You Are"

1. Gary Paulsen, *Caught by the Sea: My Life on Boats* (New York: Delacorte Press, 2001), p. 7.
2. Rachel Buchholz, "The Write Stuff," *Boys' Life*, December 1995, pp. 28–32.
3. *School Library Journal*, December 1989, <http://syndetics.com/index.aspx?isbn=0531058050/SLJREVIEW.HTML&client=milwp&type=rn12> (April 1, 2006).
4. Gary Paulsen, *Pilgrimage on a Steel Ride: A Memoir About Men and Motorcycles* (New York: Harcourt Brace & Co., 1997), p. 1.
5. Ibid., p. 2.
6. Gary Paulsen, *Hatchet* (New York: Simon & Schuster, 1987, Aladdin Paperbacks edition October 1996), inside back cover.
7. Lori Atkins Goodson, "Singlehanding: An Interview with Gary Paulsen," *The ALAN Review*, Winter 2004, <http://www.findarticles.com/p/articles/mi_qa4063/is_200401/ai_n9385111> (April 1, 2006).
8. Gary Paulsen, *Guts: The True Stories Behind Hatchet and the Brian Books* (New York: Delacorte Press, 2001), p. 121.
9. Jim Trelease, "Author Profile: Gary Paulsen," March 8, 2006, <http://www.trelease-on-reading.com/paulsen.html> (April 1, 2006).
10. Gary Paulsen, *My Life in Dog Years* (New York: Delacorte Press, 1998), pp. 1–2.

11. David Gale, "The Maximum Expression of Being Human," *School Library Journal*, June 1997, pp. 24–29.

12. Paulsen, *Pilgrimage on a Steel Ride*, pp. 22–23.

13. Paulsen, *Caught by the Sea: My Life on Boats*, pp. 78–82.

Chapter 2. Wartime and a Military Family

1. Gary Paulsen, *Eastern Sun, Winter Moon: An Autobiographical Odyssey* (New York: Harcourt Brace Jovanovich, 1993), p. 1.

2. Gary Paulsen, *The Cookcamp* (New York: Orchard Books, 1991), p. 28.

Chapter 3. Escaping From Troubles

1. Leonard S. Marcus, ed., "Gary Paulsen," *Author Talk: Conversations With Judy Blume* [et al.] (New York: Simon & Schuster, 2000), pp. 76–82.

2. "Transcript from NYPL's Author Chat with Gary Paulsen", July 9, 2003, <http://summerreading. nypl.org/read2003/chats/paulsen.cfm> (April 2, 2006).

3. Marcus, p. 77.

4. "Questions and Answers With Gary Paulsen," *Read*, August 27, 2004, p. 15.

5. Gary Paulsen, *Father Water, Mother Woods: Essays on Fishing and Hunting in the North Woods* (New York: Delacorte Press, 1994), xii.

6. Marcus, p. 77.

7. Gary Paulsen, "It Could Happen," *Read*, August 27, 2004, p. 10.

8. Gary Paulsen, *Tracker* (Scarsdale, N.Y.: Bradbury Press, 1984), p. 25.

9. Paulsen, "It Could Happen," p. 10.

10. Ibid., p. 13.

11. Jim Trelease, "Author Profile: Gary Paulsen," March 8, 2006, <http://www.trelease-on-reading.com/paulsen.html> (April 1, 2006).

12. Paulsen, "It Could Happen," p. 14.

13. Lori Atkins Goodson, "Singlehanding: An Interview With Gary Paulsen," *The ALAN Review*, Winter 2004, <http://www.findarticles.com/p/ articles/mi_qa4063/is_200401/ai_n9385111> (April 1, 2006).

14. Gary Paulsen, *The Beet Fields: Memories of a Sixteenth Summer* (New York: Delacorte Press, 2000), ix.

15. Gary Paulsen, *Tiltawhirl John* (Nashville: Nelson, 1977), p. 31.

16. Paulsen, *The Beet Fields*, p. 125.

17. Paulsen, *Tiltawhirl John*, p. 126.

18. "Gary Paulsen," *Authors and Artists for Young Adults*, vol. 7–26, Gale Research, 1992–99.

Chapter 4. Finding Himself

1. Gary Paulsen, *Winterdance: The Fine Madness of Running the Iditarod* (New York: Harcourt Brace, 1994), p. 83.

2. "Gary Paulsen," *Authors and Artists for Young Adults*, vol. 7–26, Gale Research, 1992–99.

3. Heidi Henneman, "Extreme Author Gary Paulsen Pushes Writing—and Life—to New Limits," *BookPage*, n.d., <http://www.bookpage.com/ 0306bp/gary_paulsen.html> (April 1, 2006).

4. Leonard S. Marcus, ed., "Gary Paulsen," *Author Talk: Conversations With Judy Blume* [et al.] (New York: Simon & Schuster, 2000), pp. 76–82.

5. Gary Paulsen, *Dogteam* (New York: Delacorte Press, 1993), n.p.

6. Paulsen, *Winterdance*, p. 62.

7. June Price, "'I Never Should Have Gotten Out of Dogs': An Interview With Gary Paulsen," *The Official Site of the Iditarod*, November 1, 2004, <http://www.iditarod.com/1-1.html> (April 2, 2006).

Chapter 5. Good News and Bad

1. Gary Paulsen, *Winterdance: The Fine Madness of Running the Iditarod* (New York: Harcourt Brace, 1994), p. 145.

2. Gary Paulsen, *Pilgrimage on a Steelride: A Memoir About Men and Motorcycles* (New York: Harcourt Brace & Co., 1997), p. 35.

3. Gary Paulsen, *Woodsong* (New York: Puffin Books, 1991), p. 128.

4. Rachel Buchholz, "My Life's Work: Author," *Boys' Life*, December 1995, p. 28.

5. Elizabeth Deveraux, "Gary Paulsen: A Taste for Adventure and an Obsessive Work Ethic Are This Versatile Writer's Hallmarks," *Publishers Weekly*, March 28, 1994, p. 70.

6. Lori Atkins Goodson, "Singlehanding: An Interview With Gary Paulsen," *The ALAN Review*, Winter 2004, <http://www.findarticles.com/p/articles/mi_qa4063/is_200401/ai_n9385111> (April 1, 2006).

7. Gary Paulsen, *Puppies, Dogs, and Blue Northers: Reflections on Being Raised by a Pack of Sled Dogs* (San Diego: Harcourt Brace & Co., 1996), pp. 71–72.

8. Gary Paulsen, *My Life in Dog Years* (New York: Delacorte Press, 1998), p. 7.

9. Paulsen, *Puppies, Dogs, and Blue Northers*, p. 11.

Chapter 6. Lifestyle Changes

1. June Price, "It's Like a Dance: Gary Paulsen Shares His Life and Iditarod Adventures With the Iditarod Teacher's Workshop," *The Official Site of the Iditarod*, March 10, 2005, <http://www.iditarod.com/1-1.html> (April 2, 2006).

2. Elizabeth Deveraux, "Gary Paulsen: A Taste for Adventure and an Obsessive Work Ethic Are This Versatile Writer's Hallmarks," *Publishers Weekly*, vol. 241 no. 13, March 28, 1994, p. 70.

3. "Gary Paulsen: Author Spotlight," Random House of Canada Ltd., n.d., <http://www.randomhouse.ca/catalog/author.pperl?authorid=23384> (April 2, 2006).

4. A. E. Handy, "An Interview With Gary Paulsen," *Book Report*, May/June 1991, p. 28.

5. "Transcript from NYPL's Author Chat with Gary Paulsen", July 9, 2003, <http://summerreading.nypl.org/read2003/chats/paulsen.cfm> (April 2, 2006).

6. Jim Trelease, "Author Profile: Gary Paulsen," March 8, 2006, <http://www.trelease-on-reading.com/paulsen.html> (April 1, 2006).

7. Gary Paulsen, *The Monument* (New York: Delacorte, 1991), p. 151.

8. "Gary Paulsen: Author Spotlight."

9. Gary Paulsen, *The Rifle* (San Diego: Harcourt Brace & Co., 1995), pp. 5–6.

10. Lori Atkins Goodson, "Singlehanding: An Interview With Gary Paulsen," *The ALAN Review*, Winter 2004, <http://www.findarticles.com/p/articles/mi_qa4063/is_200401/ai_n9385111> (April 1, 2006).

11. Gary Paulsen, *Pilgrimage on a Steelride: A Memoir About Men and Motorcycles* (New York: Harcourt Brace & Co., 1997), pp. 111–112.
12. Gary Paulsen, *My Life in Dog Years* (New York: Delacorte Press, 1998), p. 136.
13. Rachel Buchholz, "My Life's Work: Author," *Boys' Life*, December 1995, p. 28(3).

Chapter 7. Sailboats, Motorcycles, and More Books

1. "Transcript from NYPL's Author Chat with Gary Paulsen", July 9, 2003, <http://summerreading.nypl.org/read2003/chats/paulsen.cfm> (April 2, 2006).
2. George Robinson, Shannon Maughan, Amy Meeker, Amy Smith, Sally Lodge, Richard Donohue, Claudia Logan, Elizabeth Deveraux, "Play It Again, Sam: Eight Long-Awaited Sequels Hope to Recapture the Magic of Their Predecessors," *Publishers Weekly*, July 26, 1991, p. 11(5).
3. "Message from the Author, Teachers Guide for *Brian's Return*", Teachers at Random, n.d., <http://www.randomhouse.com/teachers/catalog>.
4. "Gary Paulsen: Author Spotlight," Random House of Canada Ltd., n.d., <http://www.randomhouse.ca/catalog/author.pperl?authorid=23384> (April 2, 2006).
5. Alice Cary, "Gary Paulsen on the Go—Sleds, Motorcycles and Sailboats," *BookPage*, November 1997, <http://www.bookpage.com/9711bp/firstperson2.html> (April 2, 2006).
6. Gary Paulsen, *Pilgrimage on a Steelride: A Memoir about Men and Motorcycles* (New York: Harcourt Brace & Co., 1997), p. 1.
7. Ibid., p. 36.

8. Ibid., pp. 86–87.

Chapter 8. "I Never Should Have Left Dogs"

1. "1997 Margaret A. Edwards Award Winner," Young Adult Library Services Association, n.d., <http://www.ala.org/ala/yalsa/booklistsawards/margaretaedwards/maeprevious/1997awardwinner.htm> (April 2, 2006).

2. Leonard S. Marcus, ed., "Gary Paulsen," *Author Talk: Conversations With Judy Blume* [et al.] (New York: Simon & Schuster, 2000), pp. 76–82.

3. "Questions and Answers With Gary Paulsen," *Read*, August 27, 2004, p. 15.

4. "1997 Margaret A. Edwards Award Winner."

5. Jennifer Flannery e-mail, March 9, 2006.

6. "Gary Paulsen: Author Spotlight," Random House of Canada Ltd., n.d., <http://www.randomhouse.ca/catalog/author.pperl?authorid=23384> (April 2, 2006).

7. "Transcript from NYPL's Author Chat with Gary Paulsen," July 9, 2003, <http://summerreading.nypl.org/read2003/chats/paulsen.cfm> (April 2, 2006).

8. Heidi Henneman, "Extreme Author Gary Paulsen Pushes Writing—and Life—to New Limits," *BookPage*, n.d., <http://www.bookpage.com/0306bp/gary_paulsen.html> (April 1, 2006).

9. Sharon Miller Cindrich, "Gary Paulsen's Love Affair With Writing," *Writer*, June 2004, p. 22.

10. A. E. Handy, "An Interview With Gary Paulsen," *Book Report*, May/June 1991, p. 28.

Glossary

abusive—Involving mistreatment or injury.

aerospace—Having to do with spacecraft or missiles designed to fly through Earth's atmosphere.

airstrip—A hard-surfaced area used as an airplane runway.

alcove—A nook or recessed part of a room.

ammunition—Anything exploded as a weapon or thrown by a weapon, such as bullets, bombs, and grenades.

amok—Out of control (also, amuck).

antibiotics—Chemicals that stop the growth of or kill bacteria and are used to treat diseases.

appendicitis—Inflammation of the appendix.

authentic—Reliable, genuine.

bounty—A reward given by a government for killing harmful animals or capturing outlaws.

craters—Bowl-shaped depressions.

desperation—Recklessness from loss of hope.

diphtheria—An infectious disease that causes weakness, high fever, and difficulty breathing.

epiphany—A moment of sudden understanding.

exhausted—Tired out; very weary and weak.

hoist—To raise, lift, or pull up.

libel—A statement that gives a false, unflattering, or damaging picture of a subject.

limelight—A position in public view, named after the kind of lights once used on theater stages.

miserable—Painful or unhappy.

overwhelmed—Overcome with emotion.

pelt—The skin of a fur-bearing animal.

pitched—Plunged or tossed with the bow and stern of a boat rising and falling.

pneumonia—Inflammation or infection in the lungs.

retriever—A hunting dog trained to find and bring back killed or wounded game.

rig—A carriage or cart.

scratched—Withdrawn from a race or contest.

sternum—Breastbone.

sympathetic—Showing agreement with one's taste, mood, or feelings.

tutor—A private teacher.

virtually—In effect although not in fact.

Selected Works

Selected Works

Culpepper's Cannon
Dunc and the Flaming Ghost
Dunc Breaks the Record
Dunc Gets Tweaked
Dunc's Doll
Dunc's Halloween
The Case of the Dirty Bird
The Haymeadow
1993   *Amos Gets Famous*
Dogteam
Dunc and Amos and the Red Tattoos
Dunc and Amos Hit the Big Top
Dunc and the Haunted Castle
Dunc and the Scam Artists
Dunc's Undercover Christmas
Harris and Me: A Summer Remembered
Nightjohn
Sisters/Hermanas
The Wild Culpepper Cruise
1994   *Amos and the Alien*
Amos's Killer Concert Caper
Coach Amos
Cowpokes and Desperadoes
Dunc and Amos Meet the Slasher
Dunc and the Greased Sticks of Doom
Father Water, Mother Woods: Essays on
     Fishing and Hunting in the North Woods
Prince Amos
Rodomonte's Revenge
The Car
The Legend of Red Horse Cavern
1995   *Amos Gets Married*

97

Flight of the Hawk
My Life in Dog Years
Soldier's Heart: A Novel of the Civil War
The Transall Saga
Thunder Valley
1999 *Alida's Song*
Brian's Return
Canoe Days
Tucket's Gold
2000 *The Beet Fields: Memories of a Sixteenth Summer*
The White Fox Chronicles
Tucket's Home
2001 *Caught by the Sea: My Life on Boats*
Guts: The True Stories Behind Hatchet and the Brian Books
2003 *Brian's Hunt*
How Angel Peterson Got His Name: And Other Outrageous Tales About Extreme Sports
Shelf Life: Stories by the Book, edited by Gary Paulsen
The Glass Cafe, or, The Stripper and the State: How My Mother Started a War with the System That Made Us Kind of Rich and a Little Bit Famous
2004 *Molly McGinty Has a Really Good Day*
The Quilt
2005 *The Time Hackers*
2006 *Bass Reeves: The Historical Account of the Most Valiant Marshall of the Old West*
The Amazing Life of Birds: The Twenty-Day Puberty Journal of Duane Homer Leech

Further Reading

Fine, Edith Hope. *Gary Paulsen: Author and Wilderness Adventurer*. Berkeley Heights, N.J.: Enslow Publishers, 2000.

Gaines, Ann. *Gary Paulsen: A Real-Life Biography*. Bear, Del.: Mitchell Lane, 2001.

Paterra, M. Elizabeth. *Gary Paulsen*. Broomall, Pa.: Chelsea House, 2002.

Paulsen, Gary. *Guts: The True Stories Behind* Hatchet *and the Brian Books*. New York: Delacorte Press, 2001.

Paulsen, Gary. *My Life in Dog Years*. New York: Delacorte Press, 1998.

Salvner, Gary M. *Presenting Gary Paulsen*. New York: Twayne Publishers, 1996.

Thomson, Sarah L. *Gary Paulsen*. New York: Rosen Publishing Group, 2003.

Internet Addresses

Gary Paulsen's Website
http://www.randomhouse.com/features/
garypaulsen/

Teens @ Random/Hang with the Authors
http://www.randomhouse.com/teens/authors/
results.pperl?authorid=23384

**Transcript from the New York Public Library's
Author Chat with Gary Paulsen**
http://summerreading.nypl.org/read2003/chats/
paulsen.cfm

Index